Much
love + gratitude

God
Gratitude
&
Giving

my experience with the
power of these three words

Melissa Bollea Rowe

God, Gratitude & Giving

Published by: Little Bird Publishing
Cover Design: Becky Reiser
Cover Photograph: Sean Rowe

First edition: May, 2022
Print ISBN: 979-8-9862431-0-8

Website: MelissaBolleaRowe.com

This book is dedicated to my son Chad Peter Smith.

Chad, may you experience the most beautiful life filled with love and full of adventure. I pray your time on this earth will be nothing short of miraculous. May you always be in good health mentally and physically. I hope you experience lots of joy, laughter, close friendships and incredible moments with the ones you love that turn into lasting memories of a life well lived. I pray you always know you are life's greatest gift to me and the reason I found the courage to chase after my dreams and find my way home. I am eternally grateful to your father for you. Raising you was such joy. Looking back it rushed by way too fast. If I could, I would do it all over again but as I finish this book you have welcomed your first daughter, "Mila," our first granddaughter into the world. My heart is exploding with joy in every way. I love you son. I am honored to be your mother. I am beyond proud of the man and father you have become. I am impressed by your character, work ethic and the beautiful life you are creating.

Sean Patrick Rowe, you are my best friend. Thank you for editing the pages of this book with me. Thank you for loving me all these years unconditionally. Words will never adequately express my gratitude for your dedication to our love story and our marriage. All the wonder in all the beautiful places I have come to discover, see, touch and experience are because of you. I believe love is the reason we are all here and I consider myself one of the luckiest people on the planet to walk through life with you by my side. I wish the whole world could know the wonderful, brilliant, kind, compassionate, generous and loving man you are. Thank you for being my compass and my lighthouse. Ours is a love for the ages.

I want to thank all the amazing teachers out there that make a difference every single day in a child's life. I've been fortunate to have had several of them throughout mine. But there is one in particular who left the most beautiful mark and everlasting impression on my heart and that was my 5th grade teacher at Kenly Elementary School in Tampa, Florida, Mrs. Gail Freeman.

Gail, I am beyond blessed to have crossed paths with you all those years ago at the very tender age of 10 years old. Your kindness, sincere words and caring heart touched mine at a time when I was hurting and needed it the most. I am grateful that I'm still able to celebrate you in my life today. What a treasure you are. I know I could not have been the only child whose life you touched so profoundly, so I will say thank you from the bottom of my heart not just for me but for all of us.

Bob and Mary Goodman, thank you for believing in me, for loving me, and for a time, on my journey through life, being honorary parents to me. You showed me the power of giving, love, acceptance and nurturing. Everyday I try to be an example of that. Your generosity and kindness will live in my heart forever. I will always pay it forward.

To my siblings Michael, Victoria and David, I love you with all my heart. I pray for you each and every day. We were meant to journey through this life together. I am honored and proud of how far we have all come.

To my family and friends I love you all. You each hold a special place in my heart.

God
Gratitude
&
Giving

my experience with the
power of these three words

Melissa Bollea Rowe

Introduction

It was years ago when I first discovered the true meaning of three beautiful words for my life: God, Gratitude and Giving. From that moment on I knew that someday I would tell the story of how these words, in this order, impacted my life and still do everyday. I am so grateful to be able to do that here in the pages of this book. My hope is that you find something of value for your life through my interpretation of their meaning.

I remember her as a little girl. Not the everyday details of her life, but a lot of it. Mostly, I remember how she felt; the things she dreamt about; the way she dissected the world around her. She was intensely curious about people. She wondered why they did the things they did and said the things they said. Adults were more curious to her because they were adults. She thought of them as possessing more wisdom and when they didn't seem to, for one reason or another, she would oftentimes think they should know better. She didn't understand it then, but her gut instincts were pretty intuitive as a child. She was what we often refer to in young people as an old soul.

Her parents were divorced. Her mother, a mom of three, worked as a waitress. They lived in an apartment and by most standards they were poor. Her father lived on the west coast. He was remarried, fighting depression and a drug addiction. She and her siblings rarely saw him. But one thing was crystal clear: in her mind, despite all of that, she was a happy child. She thought she was rich and she loved her life.

Looking back now it's easy to see she was blessed with a view of the world that seemed to be naturally positive. She thought her free lunch at school was because the world was kind. She thought she lived in a castle because her home was always neat, clean and pretty. She felt like a princess in all the pretty dresses she wore.

Birthdays were fun, special and exciting. Her birthday cakes were always chocolate with sprinkles, and she got to bake them in the kitchen with her mom. Birthdays included her brother and sister and a few neighborhood friends. Her mother filled coolers with popsicles, wrapped hotdogs in foil and kept them in the oven to stay warm for everybody, and there were always lots of balloons. Sometimes her birthday included a sleepover, with two or three friends, and her favorite game, Twister.

On the long hot summer days growing up in Tampa, Florida she spent her free time playing outside with her big brother and little sister, mostly in the water hose or in the sprinklers. A few of her neighborhood friends were older than her but she loved playing with them too. She looked up to them and enjoyed their company. All the girls wore tall knee-high socks with stars on them, had baby carriages, Easy-Bake Ovens and pogo ponies. They rode bikes up and down the street and when they got tired, they enjoyed conversations over watermelon and braided one another's hair. Many days she, her brother and sister, along with all the neighborhood kids played tag for hours and stayed out until just before dark.

She remembers feeling the happiest when listening or dancing to music. She loved it more than anything else. At home and in the car, her mom always had music playing. Music was the thing that made her think and feel the most. She can recall driving with the windows down, and the music playing all the way to the beach, on most weekends. Especially then, because the beach was her mom's favorite place to be. She would pack them Cuban sandwiches, sodas, Munchos and they would spend the entire day there.

There were so many days she can recall coming home from school and finding her bed freshly made, with a small treat from her mom on the pillow. Sometimes it was a note, a piece of gum, a quarter or a pack of M&M's, but no matter what, she always left something on the pillow. Sometimes she and her little sister would find a new pair of matching shorts or sundresses. She remembers getting a yellow polka-dotted bathing suit because she loved polka dots and yellow was her favorite color. Looking back now there's no doubt that her clothes came from a Goodwill or Kmart discount store, but that never crossed her mind. The only thing that crossed her mind was a big ole smile. She felt so much joy, peace and contentment back then. But the most memorable gift she received from her mom was a little pink bottle of "Sweet Honesty" perfume from Avon. A scent that to this day, brings back the most precious memories of her childhood.

She very much loved her mom, her life, her siblings, friends and school. Learning was fun; everyone was so interesting to observe and talk to. She loved to talk about life in particular. She felt she knew about life.

One afternoon she gathered several kids from the neighborhood into her living room without telling them why she had invited them in. Then she summoned her mom to the bathroom privately and asked if they could all live with her. She told her mother that she wished for them to have a happy life and a mother just like hers. Her mom responded by saying "Honey, these kids probably love their mother as much as you love me, did you ask them if they wanted to live with us?" To that she felt puzzled. It never crossed her mind that those kids might be just as happy as she was in their home. She hugged her mom, walked out of the bathroom and told the kids they were free to go.

While happy was the norm for her, she was an intense little girl and did a lot of thinking. On occasion, her thoughts frightened her. She didn't like that her mom mostly had to work night shifts as a waitress. She also didn't like her mom's boyfriend. He was mean. Although he tried to win over their affection with gifts, she didn't trust him. He and her mother argued often. Though she wasn't sure what their arguments were about, she can recall hearing him scream at her a lot.

She used to do the math of her mother's age, which was thirty three, at the time. She thought to herself that her mother was too young to have three children ages seven, ten and twelve years old. She worried about how her mom was going to raise them, not realizing that at ten years old, she was already half-raised.

She remembers one night she woke up and walked into the living room where she found her mom sitting on the couch. She hopped up on the couch, snuggled up next to her and said, "Mom, I'm scared that something is going to happen to you." Without hesitation her mother responded, "Sweetheart, you have nothing to worry about. I'm gonna be here to watch you and your kids grow up."

With that, she instantly felt better. She had never thought about having children of her own someday, but hearing her mom say that gave her a kind of peaceful reassurance of the future that night. But sadly, that worry in her heart was something bigger and deeper, and that something bigger and deeper was about to rear its ugly head.

On July 27, 1978, just a few weeks after that conversation, her mother, Martha Alfonso Bollea was gunned down and killed by her jealous boyfriend. No doubt little Missy, along with her brother and sister, were about to grow up fast—faster than they ever wanted to.

Though she remembers her father as a very kind and gentle man who called, and wrote letters on occasion, he had just had another child with his new wife. He never quite got his act together enough to come rescue her and her siblings after her mother died. In fact, he seemed to struggle even more with the news of their mother's passing, and would later overdose in a lonely hotel room—never coming to terms with his addictions and his own struggles in life.

From those days forward she wept every night as she lay down to sleep. She cried for what seemed like years, well into becoming a teenager. She needed her parents and they were gone too soon.

I know this little girl well: what she felt, who she was and who she became, because I am her. I still hurt for her so much. I hurt for the day our mother died, the day our father died and every day in between since. I remember my brother and sister and the confusion in all of our hearts, not just in the backseat of that long car ride to the hospital the night she was gunned down, but the many years after filled with pain and struggle without her. We moved constantly, shuffled between aunts and uncles and grandparents until ultimately we were separated from one another. I still grieve for that part of our lost childhood.

Somehow in my remaining elementary school years and throughout middle and high school I was a good student. I got good grades. In middle school I was bussed every Thursday to The Learning Center. This was a program I was enrolled in for gifted students, whose eligibility was determined through IQ testing. At that time I was twelve years old and I was told that my IQ was 146. I had no idea what that meant; I just knew school was easy for me. It was life that was hard.

As a teenager I struggled; I felt scared and alone. At times I slept in my car, got into trouble, dated the wrong guys and skipped a lot of school. I always had too much, far too much, on my mind. I worried about things like lunch money, gas money and getting a job. I worked hard to hide my struggles. I accomplished things like making the Dancerette team my senior year and being on the school newspaper staff, but throughout my high school years I was mostly depressed.

It's a wonder, looking back, that I even made it through those years, let alone got a degree from a private business college while I was pregnant. But luckily I did because, a few years after high school, I was married and had my first and only child.

While my son Chad brought me so much joy, I continued to struggle for many years emotionally. Throughout my life I would find peace in being still, in journaling, in writing poems and lyrics that, even as a child, I can recall hearing in my head. So I continued to do so until eventually, and many years later, I found my gift and my passion was in songwriting.

I followed my dreams all the way to Nashville, Tennessee. And as incredible as that was and continues to be, that's not what this book is about. This book is about something more incredible. It's about the human spirit and how I never completely lost sight of the light deep inside of me as a child. This light would ultimately lead me through, and back to, the hope-filled spaces that still existed within every other space I lived in for so many years after.

Chapter 1

GOD

There are many definitions and translations of what God is to each of us. Most of us think of God as depicted in the Bible: God Almighty, Lord, Father, El Shaddai, Abba, Mighty Creator, God Most High, Yahweh, Jehovah, Prince of Peace, Mighty Counselor, and more.

In my experience, I know God to be love, the awe-inspiring, magnificent, mysterious, beautiful divine that lives within each of us, mystifying and governing all of creation. Everything beautiful, hopeful, magical, boundless, pure and positive. A transformative energy so beautiful that if you allow yourself communion with, can heal, create and guide you through the most incredible journey of your being—life.

I witness God in everything and in every person I meet but I connect with God in silence. For that reason, this chapter will focus mostly on silence, the place I go to experience God intimately every day.

Years and years ago, as a child after my mother died, when I wanted to feel close to her I would go somewhere quiet and sit alone. I would close my eyes and ask God to see her. I would pull her as close to me as possible. So close that it was as if she was right there. I could sense everything about her: her scent, her hair, her skin, her eyes, her smile, her warmth and her touch. It gave me so much comfort. It was transformative and healing. I didn't realize it as a child, but it was then that I first created a space where silence was a place I could go to and from, and always felt the presence of not just my mother, but God.

To experience all that is infinite and eternal you must experience God. To experience God, you must become silent and to experience silence, you must become still. Can you imagine experiencing all that is infinite and eternal? Can you imagine the ways in which you might begin to experience life through the lens of an infinite and eternal love? I have and I believe you can. In the next few pages I will try to break it down for you and share some of my experiences past and present.

I crave silence. No headphones, no audio telling me how to breathe, sit, or hold my hands. Just silence. When I moved to Nashville, Tennessee in 2007, I was lucky enough to find a condominium unit in a high-rise, on the 6th floor, up on a hill. It had a balcony that was very peaceful and quiet. It overlooked the city on one side and a state park on the other.

I didn't appear to be doing anything out of the ordinary, outside of my usual time with God at sunrise one morning which back then, was not a daily routine, but it was a regular one. While sitting still and becoming silent, all of a sudden I was presented with three words: God, gratitude and giving. I knew instantly they were special. I knew they would have a profound meaning for my life and the power to transform my life. Starting first and foremost GOD. I don't know how I knew; I just did. That moment literally lit a spark in my soul. I will never forget that moment when everything shifted for me.

"I understood the message in the words to be: that if I shifted my focus daily to God, Gratitude and Giving, there would be no room for the usual fear, anxiety and worry that typically filled my days."

I used to worry a lot. To some degree, I still worry. I worry about my son, my husband, my siblings, family, friends, etc. In part, I think it's a natural thing to do, but I don't think it's natural to let worry consume you. There was a time when I was so consumed with worry. In every facet of my life, worrying was my daily routine.

I was divorced at a young age from my son's father and, many years later, living in Tennessee, I didn't feel emotionally close to my family. I didn't feel I had anyone to share my burdens or worries with. In my mind, even though I had a few close friends, I wasn't comfortable talking to them about the deepest parts of myself or my past. I had a hard time with all the memories of a difficult past, but I did a good job of keeping up a positive exterior.

While I had found comfort in being part of a church family and worship team back in Florida, years before moving to Tennessee, I had not yet found a church in Nashville. Becoming still and finding God in silence always felt like home and so I began doing it more and more often.

At the time, my son Chad was 17 and finishing his senior year of high school. I certainly wasn't going to let him know I was struggling and not feeling in control of my life. After all, I was his mom and I felt I needed to be strong; he very much still needed me.

He had not moved to Nashville with me, something I had hoped might happen after he graduated. But he was dating a beautiful girl named Lila and he had friends, family and his father in Florida. So while I went back and forth just about every weekend in the beginning, and he came to visit me often, moving was not something he was interested in doing.

How could I blame him? This was my dream, and while I did everything I could to be there for him emotionally as well as financially (even if it meant I did without) it wasn't enough in my heart. I underestimated how much I would miss not seeing or speaking to him every single day. He had begun experiencing some difficult times of his own and I contemplated moving back all the time, but sadly I didn't have enough savings to figure out how. All of this added to my worry and soon I fell into a deep depression.

Through it all, somewhere buried in my heart, was the smallest flicker of hope that someday things could, and would, get better. That seeing this dream of songwriting through would make life easier, and make me happier, so I worked hard and spent time in silence with God each day.

Through my silence I found out I was wrong—not about the smallest flicker of hope, but about a career in songwriting making me happier and making life easier. As much as I love music, as beautiful as my life has been following the dream in my heart, that was not the gift that would bring me complete joy and peace. The gift that would bring me complete joy and peace was in finding my way back home to be near my son, to a love and a family and realizing that only love gives me the most fulfillment and appreciation for all that I have and always will. Through my time in silence with God it became clearer and clearer.

When you close your eyes and think about the people and places that bring you the most peace, love, and joy, are they in your life as often as you'd like them to be? Do you get to spend enough time with them? Is there anything you can do to change that? Take a moment to write down some of your thoughts on these things and maybe plan a trip today, or create new traditions or vacations together.

Journal

_____

_____

_____

_____

_____

_____

_____

_____

_____

_____

_____

_____

_____

_____

_____

_____

_____

_____

_____

_____

_____

_____

Over the years, I had become good at sitting in silence to sort out many of my emotions when I felt I needed clarity, because silence for me is a place where I am not focusing on any outside distractions. I am not defining, judging, observing, reading, or doing anything other than quieting my internal dialogue. I do not wear headphones that tell me to breathe or relax. That does not mean I don't enjoy those things from time to time, I do. I just prefer complete silence. Sound therapy and music therapy are also very powerful practices that I have enjoyed, but they are in addition to the silence that I find so necessary.

It took a lot of practice to become silent and slip into a beautiful space of all I am and all that exists in my center. This point for me was, and is, an awareness of oneness; the most incredible feeling. In this quiet uninterrupted place, I feel the presence of God. I know the presence of God.

If you use guided meditation to get you to a place of silence then that may very well be fine for you. I would just encourage you to try to go into the silence on your own, unplugged from anyone and everything. If in the beginning all you can do is be still for ten minutes, ignore your phone or computer, and focus on your breathing, then that's a good start. Do your best to remove all distractions.

I know firsthand it's not easy at all to drown out sounds around us. It's okay to take in the natural sounds around you when you can't avoid them. It is my experience that the brain knows what to do with them and you will eventually shut them out.

Take nature for example, say you sit outside or go to the park to be still on a blanket under a tree. While on the surface we don't know how to translate natures' sounds, like a bird's song, we do know it's beautiful and it is my belief that our brains know what to do with the sounds of nature. I believe it has a deeper understanding of nature, that manifests as knowledge, when you slip into silence. This is strictly my opinion; I have not done any research on this. *It all comes back to my experiences of God, and that silence is anything but empty. I have found that it's full of answers.* It has a way of bringing clarity to what we perceive as confusion about things, people, places and situations in our lives.

> *"It all comes back to my experiences of God, and that silence is anything but empty. I have found that it's full of answers."*

I know many people may think they cannot sit in silence, or that they simply do not have time, but I have found it to be essential. I believe anyone can steal five or ten minutes every day to become silent. And in that stillness, over time, to become aware of what you are thinking and feeling so profoundly that it shifts your life in a beautiful way.

I love that the words "hear" and "art" are contained in the word "heart". I find that in the silence it is easier to hear with your heart. After all, your heart is so much more than an organ that will beat for you your entire life. Your heart is part of the beautiful divine guiding you.

Prior to your silent time, allow the energy of God and silence to become present. Relax, take several deep breaths and listen to your heartbeat. You can even place your hand over your heart. I like to do this as a comfort and acknowledgment that my mind, body, and soul are one with God, starting with my heart.

I will admit, initially it can be difficult, even funny, because in the midst of practicing silence we can suddenly begin to download things in a way that makes us want to jump right up and write them down, or fix the thing we just remembered. In the beginning of learning to become still and silent you can instantly feel anxious or silly. Either way, the key is to be patient and go through the awkwardness of, "Is this really working and what am I doing besides talking to myself?"

Just remain silent. You will no doubt be taking in the sounds around you and desperately trying to quiet your self-dialogue but, again and again and again, hang in there and try not to fall asleep. Pay attention to you: your heart, your body, your breathing, your thoughts.

Answers will come quietly, like a beautiful stranger you weren't expecting, knocking on the door. Resolve will come to that nagging commitment you wish you had not said yes to. Suddenly you'll realize that your true self said "NO" to it long before you uttered the word "YES" out of your mouth.

> *"It is my belief that when you become one with God, you have no choice but to experience the truth."*

I have made some of my biggest leaps of faith and discoveries in my times of silence. Eventually if you will just be consistent and patient with yourself, while learning to become silent, I believe you will too.

As you observe your true nature more and more, you will also observe God in and all around you, more effortlessly, outside of silence. You'll begin to notice more things about our world that are breathtaking and why it all matters is because it takes your focus away from worrying, worthless worrying.

I'd say 90% of all my worry was A) in advance, which is ridiculous, and B) false because usually the things I worried about never came to pass. The things I associated with my worry were just a waste of precious time. And time is precious. Eliminating worry through silence with God can take your mind off of the fear and anxiety you were feeling and transfer it to a place that is filled with comfort, joy and clarity.

If you think I'm suggesting that you quit worrying, sit down, be quiet and still, because it will solve most of your problems—I am. What I won't say is that it will solve them overnight, it won't. Our brains are complex organs. I believe they are miraculous organs that we can program to think and act differently. But this takes conscious effort, and it may take some time.

What I'm offering here, from my experience, is to give it a try. Once a day for five or ten minutes. Twice a day would be even better. Once in the morning when you awake, and once at another time of the day when you feel like you have to stop what you are doing and just "be still." One of my favorite verses in the Bible is in Psalm 46:10, "Be still and know that I am God." Wow, eight words that speak a million things to me now.

Being still has led me to noticing so much more. Noticing how beautiful this world truly is. Being still has led me to noticing more of my surroundings, like someone walking past me and sending them a silent prayer just because, which is probably one of my favorite things to do. I don't know why except that it feels exceptional each time. Saying a small prayer for a stranger who has no idea you just did is life energy to me, it's powerful and it's something I will talk a little more about in "Giving." After a while every little still thing becomes amazing and magical. Being still I have become so aware of the fact that only love matters.

To some degree, I know we all know this, but have we soaked it in enough to the point that we don't take it for granted, as often as possible? That we live our lives every moment understanding that we only get one life?

"Just one life. Why are we not running like we are on fire chasing our wildest dreams and living our very best lives with the ones we love?"

Earlier, I mentioned that to experience all that is infinite and eternal you must experience God. To experience God, you must become silent and to experience silence, you must become still. Can you imagine experiencing all that is infinite and eternal? Can you imagine the ways in which you might begin to experience life through the lens of an infinite and eternal love? I have and it's almost too beautiful. In what ways do you think your life might begin to shift if you experienced love every single day intentionally?

There are many ways your life will shift, and they will come to you in times and ways that are unique to you, just like they have come to me in times and ways that are unique to me. I want to share with you a shift that happened during one of my daily routines of silence not too long ago.

I have dealt with extra weight for most of my adult life and decided to take the issue of my "weight" to God, into my silence one day. Why I had not done that sooner, I don't know. But once there, I began to ask "why do I carry this weight? I felt as if my life was finally balanced in other areas, that I had followed my dreams. I was happily married and now back in Florida near my son and family.

So why is my body still holding onto weight? I had exhausted myself casting the blame on things like my thyroid, metabolism, hormones and lack of time. None of the blood tests I ever took came back with internal issues as the culprit. I was always told I was perfectly healthy, except for my weight.

As I sat in silence, deep silence, that day asking for clarity about my weight, I felt a profound whisper in my heart. The message

I felt from God was, "Melissa, no one is hurting or abusing you anymore. Yet you have continued to abuse yourself."

What? Whoa, and I mean whoa. I'm abusing myself? I remember thinking, what a harsh word, abuse. Why? I asked, why would I do that? Well, the answer came too. For many years I had unhealthy relationships, stress and worry, along with unhealthy thinking which, without realizing it, kept "weight" on me. Now that none of that existed in my life, or very little anymore, I continued out of habit and subconscious decision-making to keep the weight on myself. I was not putting myself and my health first.

I guess what I'm saying is in a lot of ways it was always me, but contributing factors I put myself in made it more difficult to manage consciously. I got used to not making myself a priority. For me, abuse of myself came in the form of carrying excess weight. Some of you may have the opposite problem, or other mental and/or physical issues.

When I tell you that discovery at that moment, was shocking, it was, but in a good way. I instantly couldn't wait to take better care of myself, starting right then. I didn't feel the dread or fear that I wouldn't be able to do it. I stopped making excuses and began devoting more time to my health and to making good choices.

I knew right away that my weight issues were gone. I really did. What it came down to was making conscious choices. It took some time to develop new habits, but I chose that day to love and forgive myself for not loving myself sooner. It simply didn't matter anymore.

I was one hundred percent ready to nurture my body. Especially now that my life was in such a good place, I was excited to fix what felt like for me the last piece of it. To be honest, I do wish I had taken that question to God sooner. But you know what? I don't care. The realization to do so came when it came and I am grateful for that day because prior to that day, I had just accepted multiple excuses for my weight. You name it, I blamed it, but not anymore.

Over the next year I made a lot of changes to the decisions of what I put in my body each and every day. I took time to shop for myself; to buy foods that I truly loved no matter what kind of preparation it took. I took the time to create fun, healthy recipes, and poured love into everything I put into my body. I lost over 55 lbs. and never looked back. I learned firsthand that food truly is life. I couldn't believe how easy it seemed once I understood that:

"To love yourself means to love what you put into nourishing your mind, body and soul every single day."

It felt exciting and still does. And you know what? I still eat carbs and sweets; I just balance my intake of them. I also love to take long walks and ride my bike. For me physical activity is important, but my biggest shift came from what I put in my mouth each and every day.

I had been nourishing my mind and soul, and finally now I was nourishing my body. I felt whole, and not just because of the food choices I made, but due to the recognition of when I ate, and what I might be feeling at that moment, so that I was eating consciously, not emotionally.

And you know what else? I was ready to finish this book. Something I had been working on for years, because I finally felt like I could stand in front of you and say, "Hey, I truly live an amazing life, mind, body and soul."

We all deserve to take the time to educate ourselves on healthy foods and have fun while doing it. I will never carry the weight of the past on me again. With every pound I lost, I closed my eyes, sat in silence and let go of a bad memory or experience. I not only lost the weight; I was shedding the weight of my past that was painful and harmful. I tied the two together and said goodbye forever.

Is weight something you struggle with? If not, what do you struggle with? Write it down here and consider taking it to silence, to God. Take a moment to become still, then honor your thoughts here. Write down whatever you feel without worry of perfection or making any sense of it for now. Just let your thoughts flow freely.

Journal

_____

_____

_____

_____

_____

_____

_____

_____

_____

_____

_____

_____

_____

_____

_____

_____

_____

_____

_____

_____

_____

_____

_____

You deserve to live with peace of mind in every way, every day. Once you master silence and what that space can reveal to you, you can set your intent on things you want to resolve there.

I consider my time of silence with God as taking it to the altar. For me that altar can be any place at all. But it can be fun to also create your own "altar" space. The most important thing in my opinion is to just find a quiet moment to be still, to be silent. You don't always have to have something you need to resolve; you can simply go there to experience God in all the glory of his good.

"It's like taking a breath mint of life."

Maybe you have a thirty minute or one-hour lunch break, but you don't have time to be silent for ten or twenty minutes, I understand. So maybe just be still for five? It can be fun. For now, let's get excited about silence and how each time you spend time there you can end it with something like, "Nice to meet ya God, again" or just a simple "thank you," which leads me to my next daily experience "Gratitude."

Chapter 2

GRATITUDE

What I know about Gratitude is that it is transformative in every way. For as much as I have practiced gratitude in my life, and for as many times I myself have witnessed others practicing gratitude, it is still not enough. There is so much I want to share and express about gratitude so let me start here.

Thank you with all my heart for taking the time to read my book. I believe one's time is the most precious gift we can give to one another. And you've decided to dedicate time to reading my book. I am beyond grateful for that. Writing it has been a dream of mine for so many years.

Ever since my life began to change from practicing gratitude daily, I too, wanted to share what a powerful and beautiful thing gratitude is. So I'll say this, and it's just my opinion but I feel as though we are either completely unaware of the power of gratitude, or perhaps we are immune to the word because we see it being crammed down our throats everywhere. I prefer to think we are still unaware somehow and just need to be reminded of this powerful practice often.

Maybe this is the time you'll find something in these words that will stick, or work for you, and you'll begin to incorporate gratitude into your life daily and find it such a blessing you'll want to share it too. I hope you will.

It's amazing to me now that I really have this gratitude thing down, how much I naturally notice missed opportunities to be grateful and it's not because I'm the gratitude police, lol I'm not. It's because I've experienced the positive impact of it so much in my own life that I just want to stop in the middle of a conversation sometimes and say, "Wait, you have so much to be grateful for; why on earth would you focus on lack ever?"

Our brains have one job, and that one job is to play the tape we give it. If you tell yourself you're miserable, scared and unhappy it says, "check", and plays that tape over and over again. Well, I'm here to suggest you try gratitude on for size and see for yourself what unbelievable things can, and will, happen when you practice it daily.

This is not to suggest that from time to time in our humanness, we won't need to complain or vent, because I sure do. But I am suggesting that once you get gratitude down you won't complain for long, or often. And, it becomes very difficult to understand, or to be around those who complain a lot.

It's funny, still to this day I will say to my husband, "Sweetheart what are you grateful for?" And always he'll say the expected things like, "I'm grateful for you, for this house, for our life, for my job." Certainly those are not bad things to be grateful for, but what I'm going for is to remind him of the not-so-obvious things, because that's where the practice of gratitude daily gets really good. If you're going to be grateful every single day, you're probably going to need to reach into your bag of gratitude often for the not-so-obvious things.

Eventually, if you begin to practice being grateful on a daily basis for even the smallest of things, you will start saying thank you for your toothbrush, the air in your lungs, a fresh loaf of bread, the bird perched in a tree near the window, the warm shower you just took, your coffee creamer, your nephew's jokes, the stranger filling your prescription who showed up at work today. It will just go on and on and that's the whole point!

"If you're so busy being grateful for even the smallest of things, something so big and transformative will start to happen."

You won't have time to focus on the not-so-great things because one, you'll get very good at being grateful which two, means you're too busy to be ungrateful to the point that three, you will do a lot less complaining because four, less complaining and more gratitude changes your mindset and overall happiness level tremendously! Don't believe me? Try it.

Ever really notice the things we complain about? Like: I'm hot; I'm hungry; I'm sick of sitting in traffic; I'm broke; there's nothing to do; my job sucks; my family sucks; I hate my body; I'm too skinny or I'm too fat; or why can't I have what he or she has; and on and on and on?

Do you have any idea how these negative thoughts affect your mood, your health and your life, over time? I'm sure there is plenty of scientific evidence to prove dis-ease, so can you imagine what shifting your perception in the opposite direction would be like for your body, mind and soul?

What if, instead the dialogue in your head played out more like: "I'm grateful to live in a world with beautiful seasons. Man I can't wait to eat; food is so satisfying, and we are so lucky to have so many food choices. I don't mind the traffic. I'm glad I have a car that runs. Things are tight but I'm grateful for my job. Maybe I can figure out some fun ways to save my money and get ahead. My family has issues but I'm learning to not let it affect me, I'm grateful for the lessons. I'm grateful for x, y and z about them. I'm learning acceptance and how to love myself more."

And what if you learned to be okay with passing days? You know, those days where you just feel kind of ho-hum. Nothing remarkable is happening so your mind starts thinking of all the ways it is dissatisfied? I call those "passing days" and try not to do too much negative thinking on those days.

Do you know that just about every single negative, ungrateful thought can be replaced with a positive, grateful one? All you have to do is get good at recognizing when you're being ungrateful and make the decision to be grateful instead. Practice makes perfect.

You will witness firsthand the magic that will take place in your life, and I do mean magic.

> *"Until you feel the miraculous effect that being grateful can have on you, you won't realize its magnitude for good, or the detrimental effect that being ungrateful has been causing you."*

Why should you start being grateful today? Because here's the thing: having an attitude of gratitude doesn't just change your life tremendously; it eventually changes the lives of everyone around you too.

You will naturally treat people kinder. You will become more aware of something about them to be grateful for, even if it's a brief encounter or conversation. In turn people will gravitate towards you and enjoy being in your presence, especially those close to you. Because as you become more and more grateful for everything in your life, inevitably you become grateful for the ones you love, and you will begin to express that gratitude towards them more which has a beautiful and positive effect on them. Which in turn comes back to you. Can you start to understand the flow of energy here?

We all have a million different perceptions of life and how we chose to live it and treat others. I'd like to share something personal with you from my perspective of gratitude and life. In the introduction of this book I shared with you that I lost my parents at a young age. Over the years and on many occasions, I have caught myself pausing to take a breath as someone happens to be walking by me in a grocery store or the mall and I hear them answer their phone and say, "Hi Mom," or "Hi Dad." In those moments, I have often wondered what it would be like to pick up the phone and hear my Mom or Dad's voice on the other end. I wonder if people who have their parents realize, or think about, how lucky they are to have their parents in their life?

"It's probably never crossed their minds that there is someone like me out there who has never once known what it's like to pick up a phone and say, 'Hi Mom' or 'Hi Dad.' "

One time in a dream, I sat around a dinner table with my parents and my siblings. I cherish that dream. I am grateful for that dream, because aside from it, I've never sat at a dinner table with my parents and my siblings all together. I'm not going for pity here. What I am wanting to share is that we all take so many things for granted. and For me it's the idea that If I could just once pick up the phone, and find my mother or father on the other end of it, that would be incredible. But that will never happen for me. So for those of you who can, maybe being grateful is in itself a gift every day to those of us who cannot.

Naturally there's a long list of things to be grateful for when it comes to our parents: or the ability to have a phone conversation with them, or buy them a gift or greeting card, all of which I have not been able to do either. I am mostly grateful that as a mother, I can talk to my son every day and that I am here for him to call.

There are also things like health. So many kids and adults deal with health issues of some kind. If you are one of the lucky ones as I am, to be in good health and to have children in good health—that, in my opinion, is reason enough to be grateful all day every day.

Life can be so hard. We all have things that we deal with emotionally, or physically, or both. Growing in gratitude can in the very least, be a way to make your day so much better. Positive energy is so powerful. I am sure there is a good amount of science on this subject but I'm not gonna go dig that stuff up for content in my book either. I am going to just repeat as much as possible that gratitude daily is life changing and I know this to be 100 percent true through my own personal experiences.

Since we spoke about silence and connection with God in the previous chapter, take a deep breath, close your eyes and if you can, be still in the present moment, try to notice the "knower" who is always present with you, your spirit, God and say thank you. Then think of a minimum ten things you are grateful for but try not to list the obvious things. Instead think of things you may not normally find gratitude in and write them down.

Journal

_____

_____

_____

_____

_____

_____

_____

_____

_____

_____

_____

_____

_____

_____

_____

_____

_____

_____

I will make a list here of things I am grateful for today:

- I am grateful for the super cute shoes I have on. They are comfortable and fit perfectly.

- I am grateful to live in the USA.

- I am grateful for the weather today. It's a little overcast and windy but I am warm and safe and inside sharing my heart with you in the writings of this book.

- I am grateful for the fresh vegetables in my salad earlier.

- I am grateful for the ability to have a grocery store close by and the money to shop for groceries.

- I am grateful for the people that go to work every day, and that make shopping available to me.

- I am grateful for my TV and internet, along with all the streaming services I get to choose fun movies from. Later my husband and I will watch our favorite series before we go to bed.

- I am grateful for iced tea. I love iced tea. I have a glass sitting here.

- I am grateful for this laptop.

- I am grateful for my garden.

- I am grateful for my home. We are blessed to own multiple homes. One is in St. Augustine, Florida. Another is in Franklin, Tennessee and two more in California.

- My home in Florida is by the beach. Before now it was just a dream. But now, I am grateful to walk outside and find the ocean at the end of my street, next to a donut shop where they bake fresh donuts daily.

- I am grateful for our mailman, he's a nice dude. He helped me find the person who stole flowers out of my yard once. Lol.

- I am grateful for this week. I've been super-focused and have gotten a lot accomplished.

- I'm grateful for next week, I know it will be amazing.

- I'm grateful for "Mila," our first granddaughter and an iPhone that keeps thousands of her photos and videos on it so that I can see her anytime I need a smile. She literally makes my heart leap.

- Speaking of smiles, I am grateful for my son's smile and laughter. When he is happy and laughs or gets excited about something, I see it on his face, I hear it in his voice, and it is the best feeling ever.

- I am grateful for my husband's job. He has the best schedule, and it enables us to spend a lot of time together.

- I am grateful for my job; I get to write songs every day.

I literally could go on and on. But I want you to know something. I didn't always have this amazing life. I attribute so much of it to the daily practice of God, Gratitude & Giving. To understand how powerful these concepts are and how incorporating them in your day-to-day life is a literal game changer you'll have to try it for yourself.

I hope that by the end of this book I will have shown you that your life is as beautiful as you believe it to be, or not. You can change the course of anything in your life right now if you choose to. There is something to be grateful for in every moment of your journey.

Journal

_____

_____

_____

_____

_____

_____

_____

_____

_____

_____

_____

_____

_____

_____

_____

_____

_____

_____

_____

_____

Chapter 3

GIVING

This subject of giving makes me so happy. It's probably the most obvious thing about my personality. I feel like giving has so much life energy in it. The day I heard the three words God, Gratitude & Giving, I will admit I zeroed in on the word "giving".

I leapt towards it curiously because I already knew it was one of my favorite things to do in this world. I instantly thought about how I would give, every single day? Would I run out of money or ideas? Then, like everything else, the act of giving daily has been even more beautiful than I could have ever imagined and no, it's impossible to run out of concepts for giving. Needless to say, Christmas is my favorite time of year.

But first, what did you give to yourself today? Did you give yourself a moment before jumping out of bed and looking at your phone? Checking your email or responding to a text message? Did you wake up and set your intention for the day before the crazy day takes over and tries to set its intention for you?

What about water, do you drink water before anything else? I know I know, it's coffee for me too but taking a sip of water first thing in the morning even before coffee just feels like I am putting something good and pure into my body first, therefore putting myself first. Water is life energy. I highly recommend you keep a bottle of water on your nightstand and drink some before bed and when you wake up.

It's the little things, it really is. What about before bed? Do you put your phone down as recommended thirty minutes before bed or like me, do you carry it to bed, lol. I am definitely a work in progress on that one, but I will say I am getting better. The fact that I'm getting this giving thing down in every other area, including myself, doesn't mean that I still don't need to keep doing some tweaking.

Remember my earlier statement when I mentioned "sending a stranger a silent prayer?" Early on I learned that if I was going to be giving every day that the act of giving would definitely not be limited to financial giving. Lord no, back then especially, I was too broke for that and I'm sure giving out nickels wouldn't have been all that effective. Although that sounds like fun. Just as easy as it is to be silent every day and express gratitude every day, so is the ease of giving every single day. So let's dive in.

I guarantee you that if you really knew how many opportunities there are in one day to "give" you'd be shocked. The next time you go to the store or out in public or at work, notice the people that pass right by you without so much as sharing a smile. I'm not saying each person you pass in life should smile at you, but you'd be surprised at how many people who do look right at you don't offer a smile. Some do but a lot don't.

These days I try very hard not to miss an opportunity to give a genuine smile to a friend or stranger. The very act of smiling can make a difference in my day and in someone's else's day. So needless to say you aren't gonna run out of smiles are you?

I don't necessarily think people who don't smile at you are rude, it's most likely just that they have a lot on their minds and it's not a conscious thing to smile often. I'm not suggesting this becomes a stressful thing by any means. I am just reminding you that we most likely miss opportunities in my opinion, to smile more often. It takes practice to make all kinds of habits, even healthy ones. It's truly a beautiful experience physically to smile more often.

More than a smile, I enjoy saying small prayers for people, even perfect strangers. Sometimes if I notice someone with a disability, or someone who appears to be going through chemo treatment or some other ailment I will say a prayer and just ask God to make their day a little lighter. Oftentimes I pray to give them relief from pain or to heal them.

For people who don't necessarily have the obvious challenges, I might send them a prayer of ease also, or I might ask for whatever unknown to me burden, that is on their heart, be lifted.

So it goes a little like this. If I see someone who appears to be frustrated, exhausted, struggling, overweight or angry for some reason, instead of judging I send her/him a prayer of peace, understanding and love. Then I offer a smile, even if it's not returned.

I always try not to appear judgmental because I find that we can all become self-conscious if we know someone is looking at us. Whether they are judging us or not, most of the time we think they are. Probably the last thing we're going to think is that a stranger is sending us silent prayers.

I'm not suggesting that I am perfect, or that in some cases it is hard to not judge situations. It is, but it's about forming different healthier habits, that in my opinion and experience, air you towards goodness. Energy is so real, so powerful.

As I said before I am not going to go dig up scientific proof of what happens in the brain when we smile, give, or laugh, and quote it here. I just know it's real. I know it's powerful. I know that this gift, the act of giving on a daily basis is like silence and gratitude—it is life changing. I've experienced it myself and still do every day.

I also love to offer up compliments as a gift to someone. I do not make up a compliment or fake a compliment, ever. But I love to genuinely compliment someone on something rather than to just think it and keep it to myself. People love compliments and I have been told many, many times that I've made someone's day by giving them a compliment.

If you are thinking, I know these things, I smile at people, I compliment them, I pray for them—then good, you are doing amazing. My advice here is to do it more often; do it daily. Give all that good energy away and watch how it comes back to you and how good it feels when it does. It will become your healthy drug of choice.

I want to go a little deeper on the giving because there really is so much on this topic I would like to try and cover. This is my first book and I know it's not going to be perfect. It's mostly going to be imperfect, but It's important to me to share how doing these things daily has changed my life. If you're still with me and you stay with me until the end I will hopefully wrap this up for you in a way that it will all make even more sense to you.

How many times have you seen something and thought, "So and so would love this," and you put it back on the shelf? Well if you can afford it, buy it. Don't put it back, make the extra effort to give it to them or send it to them. You really never know how receiving something for no reason, at the right moment or any moment, will make someone's day or change someone's week, month or year. Giving is that beautiful.

I have become much better at listening to my friends and family as a result of wanting to give more. For example, say I'm with a friend and she says something like I broke my favorite frames yesterday. Well, I may not be able to go out and purchase her a new pair of frames because it's too personal. But I can send her a gift certificate. Or I can send her a Starbucks gift card for $10 and say, "Hope your week gets better. Have a cup of coffee on me."

Why not make a list right now of things to give this week, material or nonmaterial? I know you can get creative. Once when I found out my nieces got a new apartment I filled a box full of simple items like cereal, Doritos, kitchen towels, coffee table books and a bunch of other fun stuff and mailed it to them. They were so surprised to get it.

And don't get me started on all the subscription boxes available these days. There are so many fun ones, but I love to create my own and think of fun themes for things to put in them.

When it comes to my husband I try to do little unexpected things for him, like buy him a pack of spice drops or jellybeans which he loves and put them in the kitchen drawer for him to find, lol. It never fails to make him happy.

Aside from all those things, I also believe time is love. And when you give of your time you are either saying I love you or I love me. Either way, time is love. If you are only giving your time to people, places and things that benefit you, then you are saying I love me. If you only give your time to people, places and things that benefit others you are saying I love you.

Givers can oftentimes tip the scale in unhealthy ways in which they don't realize are taking too much from themselves and, most likely people closest to them, in the process. It is so important to recognize where your giving meter is. Do you do too much for yourself and not enough for others? Or do you do too much for others and little for yourself?

The idea is to love yourself and others in a healthy, balanced way. If you are unsure, at the end of the day, make a list of what you did for you and what you did for everyone else that day and adjust accordingly. It's true that in order to be able to give to others you must give in healthy ways to yourself first. I still struggle sometimes with this. So again make a list for the next few days and at the end of your day to see if you can notice your giving patterns.

I have learned this lesson well. I am a giver. I love to give. I have to monitor my giving, my giving of my time, my giving of my money, my talents. I have a generous heart when it comes to giving and there is nothing at all wrong with that except that I believe there must be balance.

So how do you balance giving when I'm suggesting in this book that you find a way to give every single day? Well as I mentioned a few paragraphs ago, a lot of giving is life energy, and it goes both ways. If you begin offering more smiles, more prayers, more compliments in your day to others, I guarantee you will feel as beautiful as the person you smiled at, prayed for, or complimented, and that's a pretty good deal.

I mean you can pray for yourself during the day just as well as you can pray for someone else can't you? You can also pray for yourself or those you love for a specific reason, or no reason at all, and there is zero harm in doing so, only good energy. Why not make a giving list with names of your friends and family and start with some giving prayers? Don't forget to put yourself on the list and say for example pray for whatever you may have going on during the coming week.

Journal

_____

_____

_____

_____

_____

_____

_____

_____

_____

_____

_____

_____

_____

_____

_____

_____

_____

_____

_____

I'll share a short story with you that is hard to share but I'm sure some of you have similar types of stories with friends or families regarding giving.

Over the years I have spent a lot of time with my nieces and nephews. I've learned all too soon how fast time flies with my own son and how fast kids grow up. So not only have I spent countless hours driving to see them, but my husband and I have spent countless dollars on airfare and summer vacations and holidays for them. We do not regret a single bit of it.

But on one occasion, I asked my brother in advance, if he would bring his boys to me. I live three hours away and their visit was to begin on a Saturday. I'll admit that I asked him on purpose, not because I didn't want to drive and pick them up, but because I desperately wanted my brother to visit me.

He agreed and I was under the impression he and my sister-in-law were going to stay the night. I had invited them to, and in all the conversations leading up to that weekend, they never told me otherwise. I was unbelievably excited to think my brother was going to give me his time by coming to visit me while also bringing his boys to stay the week with us. My husband and I bought burgers for the grill and much more.

As it turned out, my brother came, but only to drop the boys off. Not only did he inform me when he arrived he was not going to be staying, but the entire time he was there I felt as though I was begging him for his time. I even talked him into a walk down to the end of my street where the beach and donut shop are.

I could tell my brother was anxious to leave, so when he left about an hour after arriving, I cried. I felt embarrassed in front of my husband. It's my opinion and probably a defensive one, but I felt that having to spend one night of his weekend with me was too big of an ask. He did drive the boys over, so I tried to remain grateful for what I could be grateful for, but I never forget how it all made me feel; like I wasn't worth his time.

I don't recall my brother coming to visit me often over the years and unfortunately he never built a relationship with my son when he was growing up. I should have probably told him by now how much these things have hurt me, but for the purpose of this book and demonstrating our perceptions around giving, I thought it was important to share how it made me feel on the receiving end. I remind myself often that we all *perceive* things differently in our lives and my brother may not see it this way at all.

I feel that most people, including myself, sometimes lack what I call self-awareness. For these reasons I try to practice self-awareness and balance my relationships in ways that are healthy. I'm not perfect and it is always a process. I love my brother and continue to try and love him without expectation because of how hard all our lives have been.

Like me and my little sister, he also endured a painful childhood losing our parents. It was one that we all have experienced the same but differently, and therefore our methods of coping have been different. So while I've had my feelings hurt by him over the years, I try to see all the good in him too. He's hard working, a good provider and has a great sense of humor.

The bottom line is that giving is tricky. They say to give without expectation and that, my friends, I have found is hard to do. Life is all about the details isn't it? I mean we all love differently right? We give differently and so it's really not fair to measure giving toe to toe. I think we just naturally want to receive love or appreciation in the ways we give love, and that is why oftentimes we find ourselves disappointed in the giving department.

There are people out there, that as long as you are giving to them, are always at your door. But when you need something in return, they run or quickly forget how much you've done for them. You feel as if you're only as good as the next thing you can do for them.

Well I have experienced plenty of those kinds of people and behaviors along my path that I consider are always on "the take." I've even experienced people who seem skeptical of my giving, as if I must have an ulterior motive. But you know what, I'm grateful because I've learned more about myself from all of those people and experiences and they've all helped to shape who I am. I am still learning to give without expectation every day.

I will say this though, if you experience people who can't be decent to you in the simplest fashion or acknowledge your actions with a thank you, maybe investing your time in them is not the best idea long term. There are too many kind and beautiful people in the world who need your love and care to worry about those who are not.

"When someone gives you their time, that is a valuable gift, and you should never take it for granted."

Find ways to give that are rich in meaning, balanced and heartfelt. My husband is such a thoughtful giver. He has taught me to be more thoughtful. He puts time into gifts he gives me, and it has had a profound effect on me.

It's not the number of gifts or things you do for a person, it's the thought and the way that gift translates in the giving that really matters. It really lets them know you know them, you listen to them, you see them. This is especially true when you give of your time to help feed the homeless or volunteer at benefits and events that matter to you and make the world a better place.

We've all heard it's the thought that counts. Well it is and sometimes that thought is small and sometimes that thought is wow. Either way there are lessons in giving that are powerful for both the giver and receiver.

Giving daily is a beautiful thing. Write a letter to a friend, send an email to say hello, bake someone a gift. I also have an app on my phone that allows me to send gifts anytime and it's awesome. I always get a message back saying, "What? Wow, thank you." or "I was not expecting that."

My hope is that your giving becomes contagious like flowers blooming in the Spring. I hope to watch the act of giving bloom over and over and over no matter what time of year it is. I used to have one goal and that goal was when I sat down to write out my bills they would all be charities. Well, I still have electric bills and the normal bills that will never go away but, I do my share of giving to my favorite charities as well. Life is beautiful, "give on."

Nowadays I still travel between Nashville, Florida and California with my husband. I am blessed more than ever with cool opportunities in my business for writing, speaking and spending time with my family. I work remotely and this gives me time to be present for them.

"There is time, it's how we choose to spend it that makes us feel as if we are fulfilled in life."

Without taking away any of the hardship my siblings and I went through as a result of growing up without our parents, I will say that I have come to the conclusion in life that . . .

"No matter what age you are, when you lose someone you love, it's always too soon."

Life is precious. In the scope of this great big universe that has been here for millions of years life really is short. So love while you can, smile as often as you can and remember...

"The most beautiful thing you can be is your age."

So love where you are in life and keep looking forward remembering that you can't change the past. Regret is natural; just don't get stuck there and miss the future that will soon be the past too. Yesterday, this moment was the future.

I'd love to hear from you. Reach out to me and let me know if this book has helped you and in what ways you have incorporated God, Gratitude & Giving into your daily life.

Melissa
mbollea@gmail.com

Journal

_____

_____

_____

_____

_____

_____

_____

_____

_____

_____

_____

_____

_____

_____

_____

_____

_____

_____

_____

_____

_____

_____

_____

Journal

_____
_____
_____
_____
_____
_____
_____
_____
_____
_____
_____
_____
_____
_____
_____
_____
_____
_____
_____

Made in the USA
Columbia, SC
13 May 2022